SCHOLASTIC

Let's Find Out

My REBUS Reader

Whose Habitat Is That?

by Joan Michael

SCHOLASTIC INC.
New York Toronto London Auckland Sydney New Delhi Hong Kong

This habitat has a lot of 

.

Whose habitat is that?

This habitat has a lot of 

.

Whose habitat is that?

This habitat has a lot of  .

Whose habitat is that?

Match each animal with its habitat.
Point to the animal and then point to its habitat.

Arctic

Desert

Rainforest

Mountain

desert tortoise

bighorn sheep

polar bear

toucan